ESSENTIAL SONGS FOR

trumpet

Available for
FLUTE, CLARINET, ALTO SAX, TENOR SAX, TRUMPET,
HORN, TROMBONE, VIOLIN, VIOLA, CELLO

ISBN 978-1-4234-5535-6

Visit Hal Leonard Online at
www.halleonard.com

Contact Us:
Hal Leonard
7777 West Bluemound Road
Milwaukee, WI 53213
Email: info@halleonard.com

In Europe contact:
Hal Leonard Europe Limited
42 Wigmore Street
Marylebone, London, W1U 2RN
Email: info@halleonardeurope.com

In Australia contact:
Hal Leonard Australia Pty. Ltd.
4 Lentara Court
Cheltenham, Victoria, 3192 Australia
Email: info@halleonard.com.au

CONTENTS

ALL SHOOK UP

TRUMPET

Words and Music by OTIS BLACKWELL
and ELVIS PRESLEY

ALL THE WAY

from THE JOKER IS WILD

Words by SAMMY CAHN
Music by JAMES VEN HEUSEN

TRUMPET

AND I LOVE HER

TRUMPET

Words and Music by JOHN LENNON
and PAUL McCARTNEY

ANYONE CAN WHISTLE

from ANYONE CAN WHISTLE

TRUMPET

Words and Music by
STEPHEN SONDHEIM

AUTUMN LEAVES

TRUMPET

English lyrics by JOHNNY MERCER
French lyrics by JACQUES PREVERT
Music by JOSEPH KOSMA

Slowly, with expression

BABY, I LOVE YOUR WAY

TRUMPET

Words and Music by
PETER FRAMPTON

BACK AT ONE

TRUMPET

Words and Music by
BRIAN McKNIGHT

BEAUTIFUL

TRUMPET

Words and Music by
LINDA PERRY

BECAUSE OF YOU

TRUMPET

Words and Music by KELLY CLARKSON,
DAVID HODGES and BEN MOODY

BENNIE AND THE JETS

TRUMPET

Words and Music by ELTON JOHN
and BERNIE TAUPIN

BLESS THE BROKEN ROAD

TRUMPET

Words and Music by MARCUS HUMMON,
BOBBY BOYD and JEFF HANNA

BORN FREE

from the Columbia Pictures' Release BORN FREE

TRUMPET

Words by DON BLACK
Music by JOHN BARRY

BRING HIM HOME
from LES MISÉRABLES

TRUMPET

Music by CLAUDE-MICHEL SCHÖNBERG
Lyrics by HERBERT KRETZMER and ALAIN BOUBLIL

BREATHE

TRUMPET

Words and Music by HOLLY LAMAR
and STEPHANIE BENTLEY

BYE BYE LOVE

TRUMPET

Words and Music by FELICE BRYANT
and BOUDLEAUX BRYANT

CALIFORNIA GIRLS

TRUMPET

Words and Music by BRIAN WILSON
and MIKE LOVE

CAN YOU FEEL THE LOVE TONIGHT

from Walt Disney Pictures' THE LION KING

TRUMPET

Music by ELTON JOHN
Lyrics by TIM RICE

THE CHICKEN DANCE

TRUMPET

By TERRY RENDALL
and WERNER THOMAS

CLIMB EV'RY MOUNTAIN

from THE SOUND OF MUSIC

TRUMPET

Lyrics by OSCAR HAMMERSTEIN II
Music by RICHARD RODGERS

CRAZY LITTLE THING CALLED LOVE

TRUMPET

Words and Music by
FREDDIE MERCURY

COMPLICATED

TRUMPET

Words and Music by AVRIL LAVIGNE,
LAUREN CHRISTY, SCOTT SPOCK
and GRAHAM EDWARDS

Moderate Pop

To Coda ⊕

CROCODILE ROCK

TRUMPET

Words and Music by ELTON JOHN
and BERNIE TAUPIN

DANCING QUEEN

TRUMPET

Words and Music by BENNY ANDERSSON,
BJORN ULVAEUS and STIG ANDERSON

Strong Rock

small notes optional

DON'T KNOW WHY

TRUMPET

Words and Music by
JESSE HARRIS

DREAM LOVER

TRUMPET

Words and Music by
BOBBY DARIN

DROPS OF JUPITER
(Tell Me)

TRUMPET

Words and Music by PAT MONAHAN,
JIMMY STAFFORD, ROB HOTCHKISS,
CHARLIE COLIN and SCOTT UNDERWOOD

Moderately

DUST IN THE WIND

TRUMPET

Words and Music by
KERRY LIVGREN

EASTER PARADE

from AS THOUSANDS CHEER

TRUMPET

Words and Music by
IRVING BERLIN

Moderately

ENDLESS LOVE

TRUMPET

Words and Music by
LIONEL RICHIE

FEVER

TRUMPET

Words and Music by JOHN DAVENPORT
and EDDIE COOLEY

FIRE AND RAIN

TRUMPET

Words and Music by
JAMES TAYLOR

THE FIRST CUT IS THE DEEPEST

TRUMPET

Words and Music by
CAT STEVENS

THE FOOL ON THE HILL

TRUMPET

Words and Music by JOHN LENNON
and PAUL McCARTNEY

FOOTLOOSE

Theme from the Paramount Motion Picture FOOTLOOSE

TRUMPET

Words by DEAN PITCHFORD
and KENNY LOGGINS
Music by KENNY LOGGINS

FROM A DISTANCE

TRUMPET

Words and Music by
JULIE GOLD

GO AWAY, LITTLE GIRL

TRUMPET

Words and Music by GERRY GOFFIN
and CAROLE KING

GOOD VIBRATIONS

TRUMPET

Words and Music by BRIAN WILSON
and MIKE LOVE

GOT MY MIND SET ON YOU

TRUMPET

Words and Music by
RUDY CLARK

A GROOVY KIND OF LOVE

TRUMPET

Words and Music by TONI WINE
and CAROLE BAYER SAGER

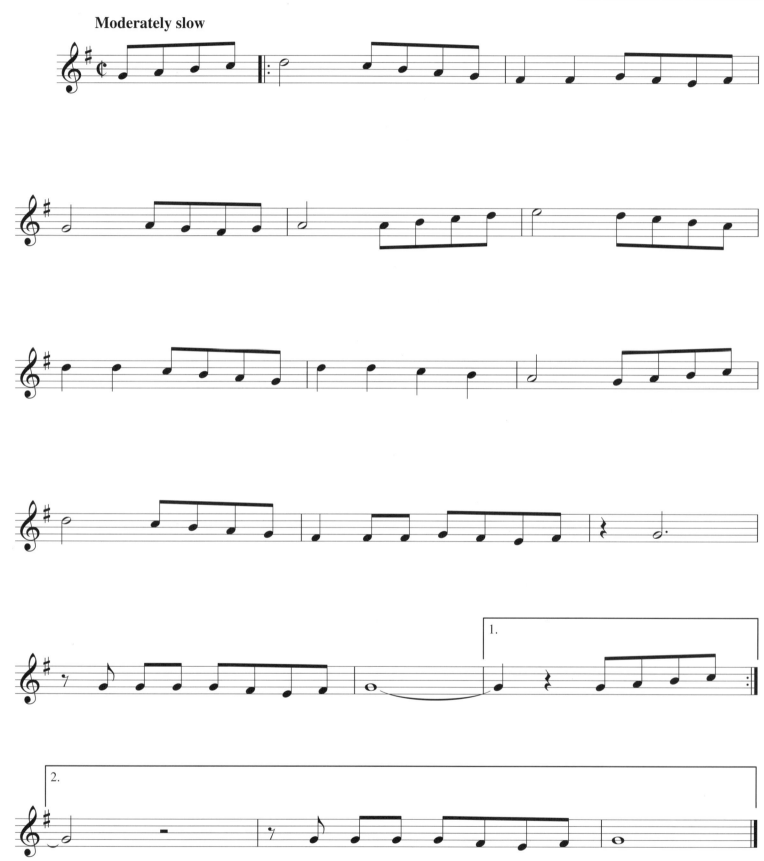

HAPPY TOGETHER

TRUMPET

Words and Music by GARRY BONNER
and ALAN GORDON

Steady, solid beat

HAPPY TRAILS

from the Television Series THE ROY ROGERS SHOW

TRUMPET

Words and Music by
DALE EVANS

HEAVEN

TRUMPET

Words and Music by BRYAN ADAMS
and JIM VALLANCE

HEAVEN

TRUMPET

Words and Music by HENRY GARZA,
JOEY GARZA and RINGO GARZA

HELLO

TRUMPET

Words and Music by
LIONEL RICHIE

HIGH HOPES

TRUMPET

Words by SAMMY CAHN
Music by JAMES VAN HEUSEN

Moderately, with a beat

HOW CAN YOU MEND A BROKEN HEART

TRUMPET

Words and Music by BARRY GIBB
and ROBIN GIBB

HOW SWEET IT IS (TO BE LOVED BY YOU)

TRUMPET

Words and Music by EDWARD HOLLAND,
LAMONT DOZIER and BRIAN HOLLAND

I GOT YOU
(I Feel Good)

TRUMPET

Words and Music by
JAMES BROWN

(Spoken:) Hey!

I HOPE YOU DANCE

TRUMPET

Words and Music by TIA SILLERS
and MARK D. SANDERS

I JUST CALLED TO SAY I LOVE YOU

TRUMPET

Words and Music by
STEVIE WONDER

I LEFT MY HEART IN SAN FRANCISCO

TRUMPET

Words by DOUGLASS CROSS
Music by GEORGE CORY

I SHOT THE SHERIFF

TRUMPET

Words and Music by
BOB MARLEY

Moderately slow, with a beat

I WANT TO HOLD YOUR HAND

TRUMPET

Words and Music by JOHN LENNON
PAUL McCARTNEY

Moderately, with a beat

I'LL BE THERE

TRUMPET

Words and Music by BERRY GORDY,
HAL DAVIS, WILLIE HUTCH
and BOB WEST

I'LL BE

TRUMPET

Words and Music by
EDWIN McCAIN

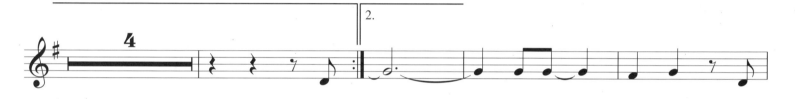

I'M WITH YOU

TRUMPET

Words and Music by AVRIL LAVIGNE, LAUREN CHRISTY,
SCOTT SPOCK and GRAHAM EDWARDS

IF

TRUMPET

Words and Music by
DAVID GATES

IF I HAD A HAMMER
(The Hammer Song)

TRUMPET

Words and Music by LEE HAYS
and PETE SEEGER

THE IMPRESSION THAT I GET

TRUMPET

Words and Music by DICKY BARRETT
and JOE GITTLEMAN

IN THE MOOD

TRUPMET

By JOE GARLAND

IT'S A SMALL WORLD

from "it's a small world" at Disneyland Park and Magic Kingdom Park

TRUMPET

Words and Music by RICHARD M. SHERMAN
and ROBERT B. SHERMAN

IT'S TOO LATE

TRUMPET

Words and Music by CAROLE KING
and TONI STERN

Slowly

ITSY BITSY TEENIE WEENIE
YELLOW POLKADOT BIKINI

TRUMPET

Words and Music by PAUL VANCE
and LEE POCKRISS

THEME FROM "JURASSIC PARK"

from the Universal Motion Picture JURASSIC PARK

TRUMPET

Composed by
JOHN WILLIAMS

KING OF THE ROAD

TRUMPET

Words and Music by
ROGER MILLER

LA BAMBA

TRUMPET

By RITCHIE VALENS

Moderate Latin Rock

LET IT BE

TRUMPET

Words and Music by JOHN LENNON
PAUL McCARTNEY

To Coda $\oplus$

D.S. al Coda

CODA $\oplus$

LISTEN TO WHAT THE MAN SAID

TRUMPET

Words and Music by
PAUL and LINDA McCARTNEY

THE LOCO-MOTION

TRUMPET

Words and Music by GERRY GOFFIN
and CAROLE KING

LOUIE, LOUIE

TRUMPET

Words and Music by
RICHARD BERRY

LOVE ME TENDER

TRUMPET

Words and Music by ELVIS PRESLEY
and VERA MATSON

LUCY IN THE SKY WITH DIAMONDS

TRUMPET

Words and Music by JOHN LENNON
and PAUL McCARTNEY

MAMBO NO. 5
(A Little Bit Of...)

TRUMPET

Original Music by DAMASO PEREZ PRADO
Words by LOU BEGA and ZIPPY

ME AND BOBBY McGEE

TRUMPET

Words and Music by KRIS KRISTOFFERSON
and FRED FOSTER

Moderately

A MOMENT LIKE THIS

TRUMPET

Words and Music by JOHN REID
and JORGEN KJELL ELOFSSON

Moderately slow

MY FAVORITE THINGS
from THE SOUND OF MUSIC

TRUMPET

Lyrics by OSCAR HAMMERSTEIN II
Music by RICHARD RODGERS

Lively, with spirit

THE ODD COUPLE

Theme from the Paramount Picture THE ODD COUPLE
Theme from the Paramount Television Series THE ODD COUPLE

TRUMPET

By NEAL HEFTI

ON TOP OF SPAGHETTI

TRUMPET

Words and Music by
TOM GLAZER

Moderately fast, with spirit

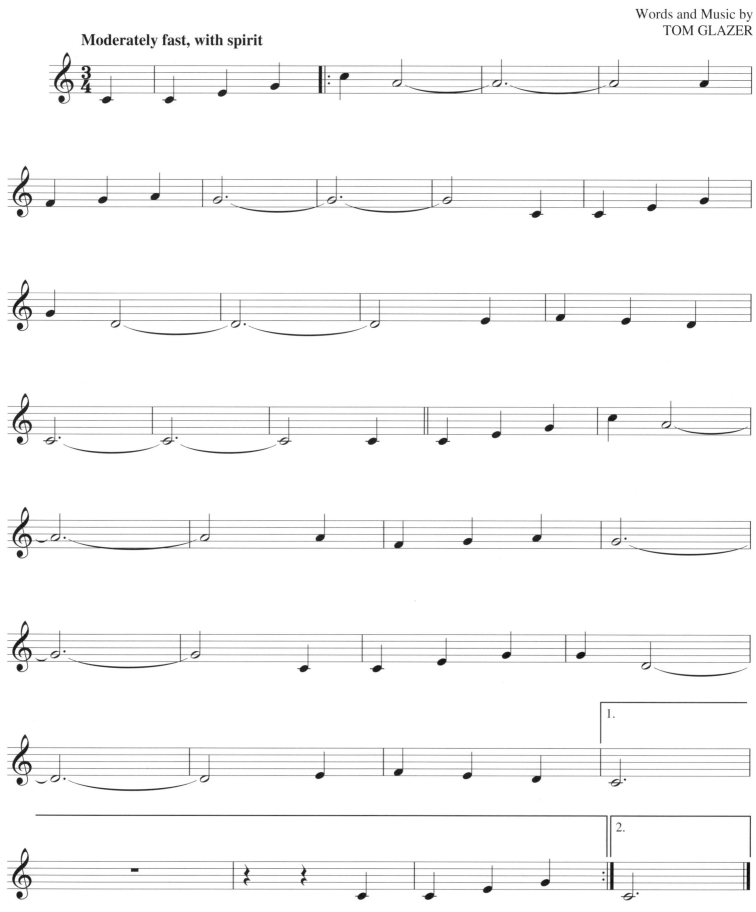

100 YEARS

TRUMPET

Words and Music by
JOHN ONDRASIK

ONE NOTE SAMBA
(Samba de uma nota so)

TRUMPET

Original Lyrics by NEWTON MENDONCA
English Lyrics by ANTONIO CARLOS JOBIM
Music by ANTONIO CARLOS JOBIM

PETER COTTONTAIL

TRUMPET

Words and Music by STEVE NELSON
and JACK ROLLINS

PUPPY LOVE

TRUMPET

Words and Music by
PAUL ANKA

Moderately slow

QUE SERA, SERA
(Whatever Will Be, Will Be)
from THE MAN WHO KNEW TOO MUCH

Words and Music by JAY LIVINGSTON
and RAY EVANS

TRUMPET

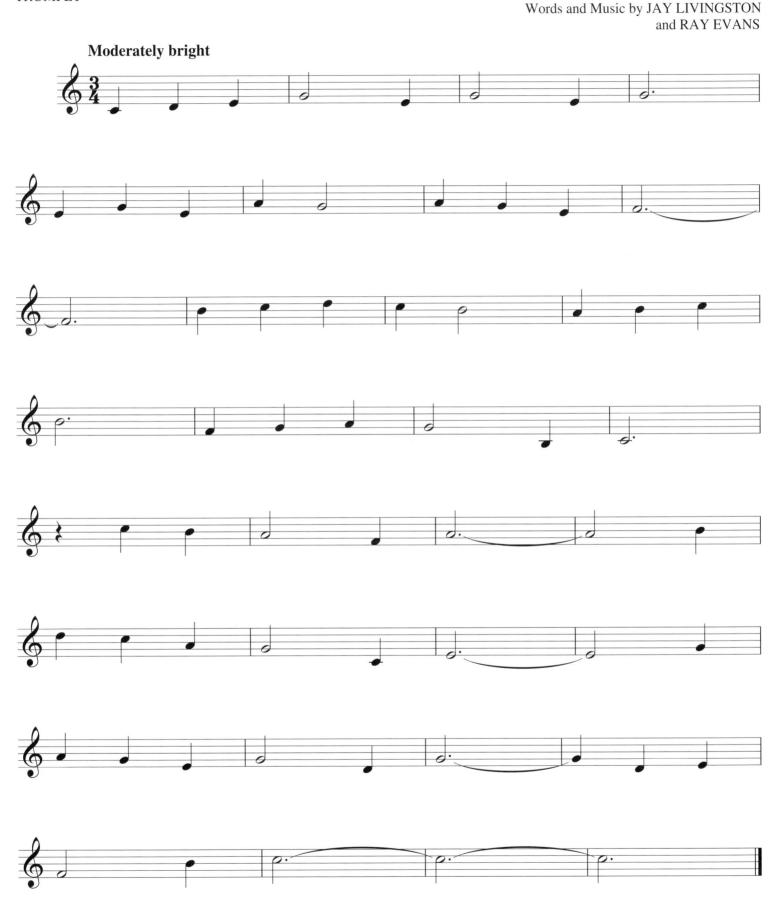

R.O.C.K. IN THE U.S.A
(A Salute to 60's Rock)

TRUMPET

Words and Music by
JOHN MELLENCAMP

Fast Rock

THE RAINBOW CONNECTION

from THE MUPPET MOVIE

TRUMPET

Words and Music by PAUL WILLIAMS
and KENNETH L. ASCHER

RAINDROPS KEEP FALLIN' ON MY HEAD

from BUTCH CASSIDY AND THE SUNDANCE KID

TRUMPET

Lyric by HAL DAVID
Music by BURT BACHARACH

ROCKIN' ROBIN

TRUPPET

Words and Music by
J. THOMAS

SAILING

TRUMPET

Words and Music by
CHRISTOPHER CROSS

SEE YOU LATER, ALLIGATOR

TRUMPET

Words and Music by
ROBERT GUIDRY

SEVENTY SIX TROMBONES

from Meredith Willson's THE MUSIC MAN

By MEREDITH WILLSON

TRUMPET

SHAKE, RATTLE AND ROLL

TRUMPET

Words and Music by
CHARLES CALHOUN

SHOUT

TRUMPET

Words and Music by ROLAND ORZABAL
and IAN STANLEY

SIXTEEN GOING ON SEVENTEEN

from THE SOUND OF MUSIC

TRUMPET

Lyrics by OSCAR HAMMERSTEIN II
Music by RICHARD RODGERS

Slowly, with expression

SMOOTH

TRUMPET

Words by ROB THOMAS
Music by ROB THOMAS and ITALL SHUR

SO NICE
(Summer Samba)

TRUMPET

Original Words and Music by MARCOS VALLE
and PAULO SERGIO VALLE
English Words by NORMAN GIMBEL

Moderately

THE SOUND OF MUSIC
from THE SOUND OF MUSIC

TRUMPET

Lyrics by OSCAR HAMMERSTEIN II
Music by RICHARD RODGERS

With much expression

SPINNING WHEEL

TRUMPET

Words and Music by
DAVID CLAYTON THOMAS

SPLISH SPLASH

TRUMPET

Words and Music by BOBBY DARIN
and MURRAY KAUFMAN

STAND BY ME

TRUMPET

Words and Music by JERRY LEIBER,
MIKE STOLLER and BEN E. KING

SUNNY

TRUMPET

Words and Music by
BOBBY HEBB

SUPERCALIFRAGILISTICEXPIALIDOCIOUS

from Walt Disney's MARY POPPINS

TRUMPET

Words and Music by RICHARD M. SHERMAN
and ROBERT B. SHERMAN

SURFIN' U.S.A.

TRUMPET

Words and Music by
CHUCK BERRY

TAKIN' CARE OF BUSINESS

TRUMPET

Words and Music by
RANDY BACHMAN

TEARS IN HEAVEN

TRUMPET

Words and Music by ERIC CLAPTON
and WILL JENNINGS

TENNESSEE WALTZ

TRUMPET

Words and Music by REDD STEWART
and PEE WEE KING

Easy Waltz

THAT'LL BE THE DAY

TRUMPET

Words and Music by JERRY ALLISON,
NORMAN PETTY and BUDDY HOLLY

THIS LOVE

TRUMPET

Words and Music by ADAM LEVINE
and JESSE CARMICHAEL

Moderate Rock

TIE A YELLOW RIBBON
ROUND THE OLE OAK TREE

TRUMPET

Words and Music by L. RUSSELL BROWN
and IRWIN LEVINE

TIJUANA TAXI

TRUMPET

Words by JOHNNY FLAMINGO
Music by ERVAN "BUD" COLEMAN

TRUE COLORS

TRUMPET

Words and Music by BILLY STEINBERG
and TOM KELLY

THE TWIST

TRUMPET

Words and Music by
HANK BALLARD

UP WHERE WE BELONG

from the Paramount Picture AN OFFICER AND A GENTLEMAN

TRUMPET

Words by WILL JENNINGS
Music by BUFFY SAINTE-MARIE and JACK NITZSCHE

WALKING IN MEMPHIS

TRUPET

Words and Music by
MARC COHN

CODA 1

D.S. al Coda 1

Suddenly slowly, freely

Tempo I

2

D.C. al Coda 2

CODA 2

THE WAY YOU LOOK TONIGHT
from SWING TIME

TRUMPET

Words by DOROTHY FIELDS
Music by JEROME KERN

WE ARE FAMILY

TRUMPET

Words and Music by NILE RODGERS
and BERNARD EDWARDS

WE ARE THE CHAMPIONS

TRUMPET

Words and Music by
FREDDIE MERCURY

WE BUILT THIS CITY

TRUMPET

Words and Music by BERNIE TAUPIN, MARTIN PAGE,
DENNIS LAMBERT and PETER WOLF

WE'VE ONLY JUST BEGUN

TRUMPET

Words and Music by ROGER NICHOLS
and PAUL WILLIAMS

WHITE FLAG

TRUMPET

Words and Music by RICK NOWELS,
ROLLO ARMSTRONG and DIDO ARMSTRONG

A WHOLE NEW WORLD

from Walt Disney's ALADDIN

TRUMPET

Music by ALAN MENKEN
Lyrics by TIM RICE

Y.M.C.A.

TRUMPET

Words and Music by JACQUES MORALI,
HENRI BELOLO and VICTOR WILLIS

YESTERDAY

TRUMPET

Words and Music by JOHN LENNON
and PAUL McCARTNEY

Moderately, with expression

YOU ARE MY SUNSHINE

TRUMPET

Words and Music by
JIMMIE DAVIS

Lively

YOU LIGHT UP MY LIFE

TRUPMET

Words and Music by
JOSEPH BROOKS

YOU ARE THE MUSIC IN ME

from the Disney Channel Original Movie HIGH SCHOOL MUSICAL 2

TRUMPET

Words and Music by
JAMIE HOUSTON

Moderately fast Rock

139

YOU'RE BEAUTIFUL

TRUMPET

Words and Music by JAMES BLUNT,
SACHA SKARBEK and AMANDA GHOST

YOU'RE STILL THE ONE

TRUMPET

Words and Music by SHANIA TWAIN
and ROBERT JOHN LANGE

YOU'VE GOT A FRIEND IN ME

from Walt Disney's TOY STORY

TRUMPET

Music and Lyrics by
RANDY NEWMAN

YOUR SONG

TRUMPET

Words and Music by ELTON JOHN
and BERNIE TAUPIN

ZOOT SUIT RIOT

TRUMPET

Words and Music by
STEVE PERRY

Spoken: Blow, dad - dy!

small notes optional

To Coda

D.S. al Coda

CODA